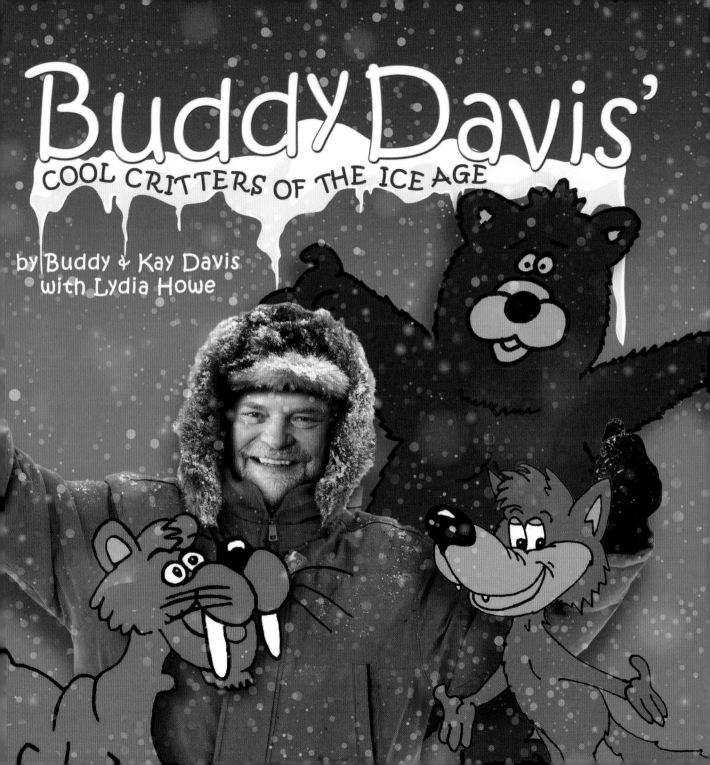

Buddy Davis'
COOL CRITTERS OF THE ICE AGE

by Buddy & Kay Davis
with Lydia Howe

First Printing: April 2015

Illustrations by Buddy Davis
Interior design by Terry White

ISBN 13: 978-0-89051-858-8
Library of Congress Catalog Card Number: 2014958519

Printed in China

Please consider requesting that a copy of this volume
be purchased by your local library system.

For information regarding author interviews,
please contact the publicity department at (870) 438-5288.

Master
Books®
A Division of New Leaf Publishing Group
www.masterbooks.net

Hi, I'm Buddy Davis, and I'll be your tour guide today as we explore some of the cool critters of the Ice Age.

This is my sidekick, Harry, the cave bear. Grab your coat, gloves, and some hot chocolate, and let's go!

Before we go and find the critters, let's talk about how the Ice Age happened.

The Flood of Noah's day covered the whole earth and created the perfect environment for an Ice Age.

In Genesis 7:11, the Bible tells us that the fountains of the great deep broke open. That means that there were volcanoes in the ocean, which would have warmed the waters.

5

At the same time, there were volcanoes on land that shot a lot of ash high into the atmosphere, creating dark clouds that kept sun rays from reaching the land. This would make the land cooler.

Some scientists believe that the Artic Ocean could have gotten as warm as 80 degrees for a short period of time.

Today if you dipped your toes in the Artic Ocean, they would freeze! I know from experience…

The evaporation, when water became steam, lowered the oceans as much as 300 feet, forming land bridges. Here Harry the cave bear is scouting out the land across the ocean.

When the land bridge formed, Harry the cave bear decided to travel from Russia to Alaska just like many other critters and even people.

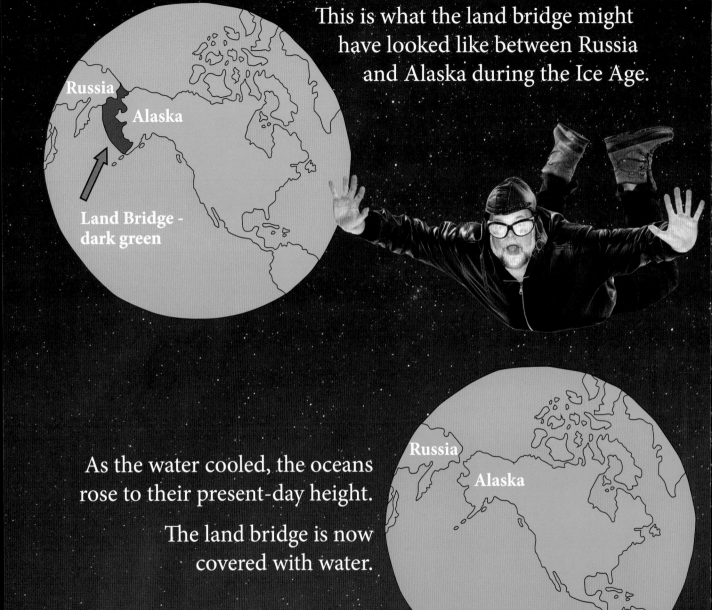

This is what the land bridge might have looked like between Russia and Alaska during the Ice Age.

Russia

Alaska

Land Bridge - dark green

As the water cooled, the oceans rose to their present-day height.

The land bridge is now covered with water.

Russia

Alaska

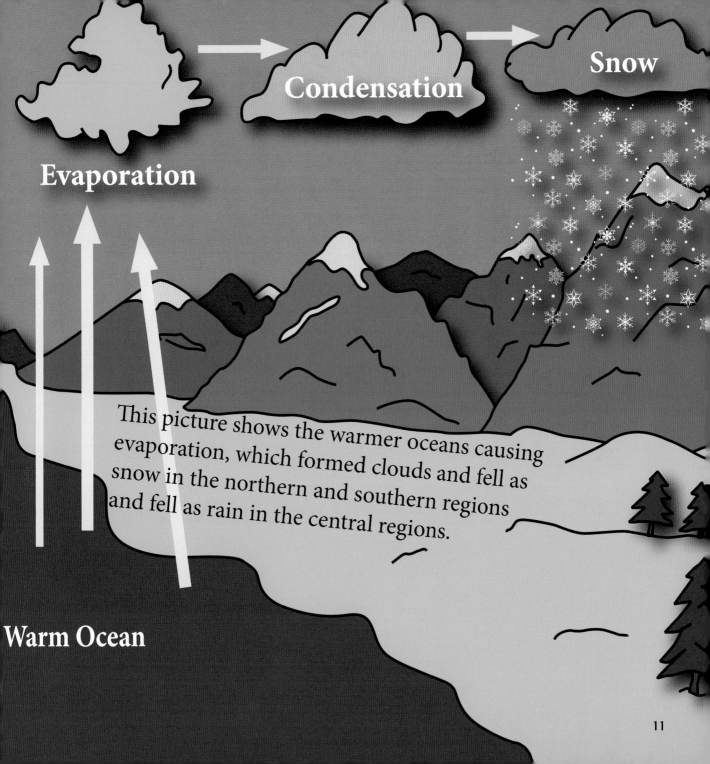

Evaporation

Condensation

Snow

This picture shows the warmer oceans causing evaporation, which formed clouds and fell as snow in the northern and southern regions and fell as rain in the central regions.

Warm Ocean

Snow kept falling and falling, eventually turning into glaciers, large, slow-moving areas of ice.

You can see how Harry the cave bear might have experienced the buildup of snow. Brrrrr, just thinking about it makes me thirsty for more hot chocolate.

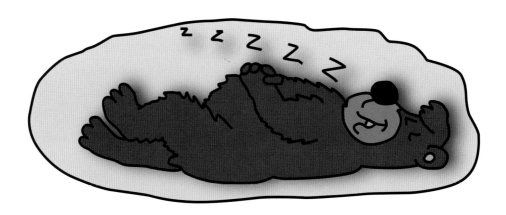

No worries! Harry the cave bear hibernated in an ice cave.

The entire world was not covered with ice. You can see by the white on the map the areas of the snow and ice. Can you imagine how cold that would be? Just thinking about it makes me shiver!

In some of the colder regions of the world today, you can still see some glaciers left over from the Ice Age.

Did you know that there are ice worms that live in some glaciers? Cool!

This is Mendenhall Glacier in Alaska. Wouldn't it be so much fun to explore?

One of the oldest books in the Bible is Job. The book mentions snow and ice. Some people believe Job may have lived through the Ice Age even though the snow and ice would not have covered where he lived. Check out Job 6:16 and Job 38:22!

Now that we know how the Ice Age happened, let's go find some of the cool critters who lived during that time.

Please note: Some of these animals have been found frozen, but many are just fossilized bones. No one knows their color or much about their appearance. Some things we have to guess on.

Strap on your skis and let's go!

WOOLLY
MAMMOTH

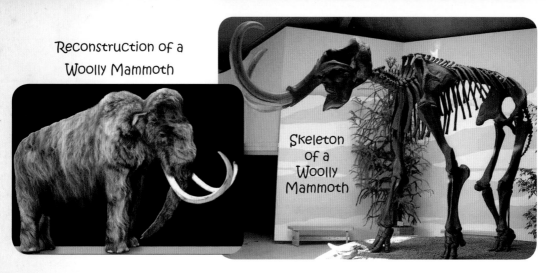

Reconstruction of a Woolly Mammoth

Skeleton of a Woolly Mammoth

Woolly Mammoths were about the size of a modern-day elephant.

The Woolly Mammoth lived in Asia, Europe, Siberia, and Alaska. Their ears and tails were smaller than modern-day elephants. This helped keep them from losing their body heat. All elephants have hair but the Woolly Mammoth had an extra thick and long coat. They had curved tusks that could reach 17 feet in length.

21

GLYPTODON

Skeleton of a Glyptodon

The Glyptodon was about the size of a small car weighing up to 2,000 pounds.

This is a fossil of Glyptodon.

The Glyptodon was an armadillo-like mammal that was covered in armor. It also had a dangerous tail full of bone spikes. This could be the original 4 wheel drive.

FEET

GIANT
BISON

Painting of a Giant Bison

Skeleton of a Giant Bison

The Giant Bison could reach up to 8 feet tall at the shoulders and could weigh over 4,400 lbs.

The first fossil of the Giant Bison was found in 1803 at Big Bone Lick in Kentucky. It is believed that they would have lived in family groups grazing the Great Plains and browsing in the woodlands of North America.

The horns of the Giant Bison measures 84 inches from tip to tip. These large horns would have kept predators away.

GIANT
BEAVER

26

Painting of a Giant Beaver

One of the few skeletons found of the Giant Beaver.

The Giant Beaver grew as large as a black bear and could weigh up to 220 pounds.

The Giant Beaver lived in North America ranging from Alaska to Florida. Very few fossils were ever found, with the first discovered in 1837 in a peat bog in Ohio. It is the largest beaver ever to exist. Their huge front teeth could be up to 5.9 inches long.

FEET

The Cave Bear could stand over 10 feet tall and could weigh as much as 1,000 pounds.

Skeleton of a Cave Bear

The Cave Bear lived in Europe and was first described in 1774. There have been several thousands of fossils of the Cave Bear found. According to the wear on the teeth, the Cave Bear seems to have been primarily a plant eater.

Reconstruction of a Cave Bear

FEET

MUSK
OX

This modern day Musk Ox looks like its Ice Age ancestors.

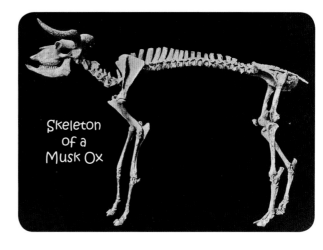

Skeleton of a Musk Ox

Musk Ox can weigh up to 800 pounds and can grow as tall as 5 feet at the shoulder.

The Musk Ox is an Arctic mammal noted for its thick coat. Males have a very strong odor for which it gets its name. When under attack, they form a tight circle, and males will rush out at the enemy.

IRISH
ELK

32

Fossil
of the
Irish Elk

The Irish Elk could grow to a little over 6 feet tall at the shoulders.

The Irish Elk is the largest deer that ever lived. Its home range was in Europe, Asia, and Africa. Most of the fossil skeletons have been found in Irish bogs. Its antlers grew to over 12 feet in length. Like all deer, the Irish Elk would shed and re-grow their antlers each year.

They grew the largest set of antlers of any deer.

DIRE
WOLF

34

The Dire Wolf
looked a lot like this
modern-day wolf.

Skeleton
of a
Dire Wolf

The Dire Wolf
averaged about 5 feet
in length and could
weigh up to
174 pounds.

The Dire Wolf was about the size of the
Gray Wolf. They were common in North
and South America and lived in a variety
of habitats. The fossil evidence suggests
that they hunted in packs like modern-day
wolves. Thousands
of fossil
remains of the
Dire Wolf have
been found in the La Brea
Tar Pits in California.

FEET

12
11
10
9
8
7
6
5
4
3
2
1

GIANT
GROUND
SLOTH

36

The Giant Ground Sloth grew up to 20 feet tall and could weigh up to 6,000 pounds.

Skeletons of Giant Ground Sloths

The Giant Ground Sloth soon found its way to North America after Noah's Flood. When feeding it would raise up on its back legs and use its powerful claws and arms to bend down the branches. This huge animal was a plant eater and believed to be a gentle giant. Its large size would have scared away most predators.

The Giant Ground Sloth would have spent most of its time walking on all fours. It would have been the size of a bison.

FEET

BALUCHITHERIUM
(bal-oo-ki-theory-um)

38

Painting of cow and calf

The skull of the Baluchitherium was over 4 feet long.

The Baluchitherium stood 16 feet at the shoulders, and the top of its head could reach 26 feet.

The Baluchitherium is considered the largest land mammal that ever lived. It is believed to be a type of rhinoceros. It was discovered in 1910 in Pakistan. This gigantic hornless rhino-like critter was a plant-eater. How would you like this gigantic beast looking in your third-story window begging for a snack?

SABER-
TOOTH
CAT

Painting of a Smilodon

Smilodon was from 4 to 5 feet long. They were smaller than tigers and African lions.

The canine teeth could grow more than 9 inches long. How would like to brush these teeth?

The best known of the saber-tooth cats was Smilodon. It lived in North America and was thought to be an excellent hunter. There were many types of saber-tooth cats. All saber-tooth cats were designed to open their jaws a lot farther than most of the big cats today. The canine teeth were like sabers, long and curved.

41

TERATORN
(TEAR-uh-torn)

Artist drawing
of Teratorns

When soaring, the monster
bird probably would have
looked like this condor.

Teratorn means "monster bird." The fossils of this extinct bird have been found in North and South America. Over 100 specimens have been found in the La Brea Tar Pits in California.

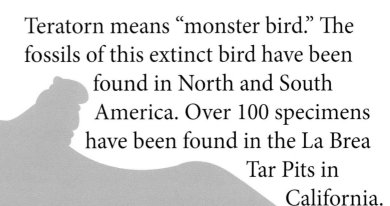

This very large extinct bird had a wingspan of 12 feet. I wonder if I could hitch a ride on him.

FEET

43

BRONTOTHERIUM
(bron-tow-THEE-ree-um)

44

Painting of a Brontotherium

Brontotherium stood 8.2 feet at the shoulders and was 16 feet long.

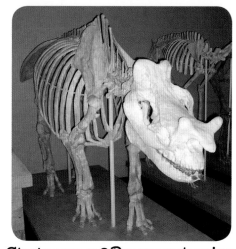
Skeleton of Brontotherium

Fossils of Brontotherium have been found in South Dakota and Nebraska. They have an unusual y-shaped horn on their nose. These animals probably lived in herds and wandered through open woodlands searching for plants.

WOOLLY
RHINOCEROS

46

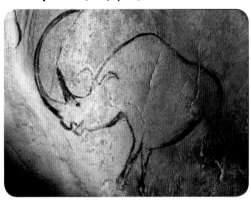

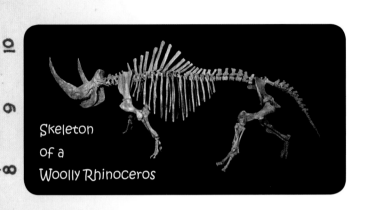

Skeleton
of a
Woolly Rhinoceros

The Woolly Rhinoceros would have stood 5 to 6 feet tall and was 10 to 12 feet long.

Woolly Rhinoceros fossils were found in Europe. These critters had huge horns on their snout, with one of them growing over 3 feet long. They had shaggy, thick coats, which helped them withstand the harsh winter conditions. They were plant eaters.

47

ANDREWSARCHUS
(AN-drew-SAR-cus)

48

Painting of a Andrewsarchus

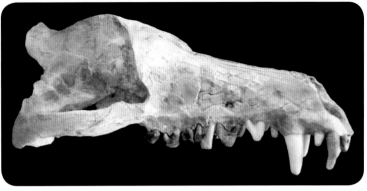

Only the skull of Andrewsarchus has been found. I wouldn't have wanted to meet this guy after dark...or in the daytime either!

With a skull that is 3 feet long, it is estimated this animal could have stood 5 feet tall or more at the shoulders.

Not much is known about this Ice Age critter. Only the skull was found in 1923 in the Gobi Desert in Mongolia. It is believed to be the largest meat-eating land mammal known. It had very large, strong teeth in its skull. Some scientists believe it was hyena-like in its appearance.

49

SYNDOCERAS
(Sin-dee-oh-sair-us)

Pencil drawings of the Syndoceras

Syndoceras grew to be about 5 feet long.

Fossils of this small deer were found in Nebraska. In addition to a pair of cow-like horns, they had a strange y-shaped horn on their nose. They also had tusk-like canine teeth used to root out food.

51

TITANOTYLOPUS
(tie-TAN-oh-TIE-low-pus)

The skull of Titanotylopus

Titanotylopus was 13 feet long and weighed up to 2,000 pounds. He grew to be 11 and ½ feet tall at the shoulders.

This camel is similar to modern-day camels. Many scientists believe that it even had a hump on its back for fat storage. Fossils of this critter were found in Nebraska. Titanotylopus was taller than most elephants.

53

What happened to the Ice Age critters?

Some died of natural causes such as environmental changes, and some were hunted into extinction.